POSTCARDS
FROM MY FUTURE SELF

BY
DEBORAH DICEMBRE

First published by Platypus Publishing 2023

PLATYPUS

PUBLISHING

Deborah Dicembre

Have you ever reached a point where you think, change is too hard?

Things just are the way they are?

Do you lose hope that you'll get a break or that things will work out?

Do you think that with your background or circumstances, meaningful lasting growth is impossible and you'll never reach your dreams and goals?

Is change so slow it's painful? No matter how hard you try, progress is not happening quickly enough? Do you get ahead only to slip back into old ways and mindsets losing all the ground you've just made? Sound familiar?

Then this is the book for you.

This is hands down the #1 mood and mindset shifter I have ever discovered.

There are no bad or wasted days when your future self is at the helm.

You walk and talk differently. You learn differently. You hold yourself differently.

It's palpable. The energy shift around you is immediate.

People notice, you notice. It becomes part of your fabric. Instantly.

Understand this: Your future self has one thing on their mind and that is, who you are NOW in this present moment.

One of the most valuable things to happen when we are our future self in the present, is that we remain seated, unshaken, unmoved in the centre of our being.

It is THE most effective, straight ahead pathway, to self mastery.

The value of this can not be overstated or underestimated.

'Whoever is slow to anger is better than the mighty and he who rules himself is greater than he who takes a city'

Proverbs 16 v 32

POSTCARDS

FROM MY FUTURE SELF

BY
DEBORAH DICEMBRE

For
Dino And Ava
and 8 year old me

'Imagination is more important
than knowledge'
- Albert Einstein

INTRODUCTION

There are only two people in this life you need to impress: 8 year old you and 80 year old you. And these are the 2 people who keep me going when all else goes to hell.

My 80 year old self is as nurturing as she is badass. Does not care what anyone thinks or says about her. She's the woman I want to be. She's a woman I want to know.

And she's a woman that's calling me forward, giving me the strength and the courage to fulfil my dreams, make courageous choices, to become all I was created to be. She knows my fears and she knows my past. She doesn't judge. Her one goal is to move me forward. And she does that so well.

8 year old me is full of dreams and wonder. She is not restricted by the limitations that slowly squeeze the imagination and life out of us all. Her heart has never been given or broken. She is complete. Her spirit is intact and her eyes sparkle like diamonds. She is fierce. No foe can overcome her. She is the heroine of every story she writes. Her mind is a fertile, water drenched, well fed garden bed. She flies with fairies on the backs of dragons. She talks to animals and they talk back to her. Flowers are her friends. She is a wealth of knowledge and

power just waiting to be tapped. She believes. She believes in herself and she believes in me.

No matter how old you are right now, we are all 8 and 80 somewhere on the time space continuum. How does future you, hold herself? What goes thru the mind of 8 year old you when she sees you now? These are the questions that are better asked than what does Mary or Joe down the road think of you. Or Jean and John at work. Mary and Joes come and go but 8yr old you and 80 yr old you are with you always. They are an infinite source of wisdom and encouragement and they are connected to the Infinite Source of wisdom and encouragement. They cheer you on. They pull you into line and over the line. They listen. They speak. One has the look of hope and belief in her eyes; the other, a strong 'don't mess with me ', confidence and the wisdom of years. These are the people of our personal inner circle.

I can only say I wish I knew these two beautiful souls years ago. Since I've been able to tap into all the goodness they have to offer, present day me has a confidence and steady consistency that yesterday me could only dream about. If me now was advising me in my 20's and 30', what a significant difference that would have made. I would have called people places and things for what they were and not been afraid to make decisions accordingly and in my best interests. As a young woman I didn't want to hurt anyone's feelings (still don't, but I don't take other people's emotional responses to my decisions personally as manipulators would have you do) And I didn't want to embarrass anyone. So I didn't call them out on their behaviour. I could see what was going on, but I froze up. Future me, does not freeze up. She calls it as she sees it and she steers me right. I have no fear in following her advice. It's solid. That's the gold. It's like being you but one person removed. No one has my back like future me.

I'm not a quitter but knowing when to quit is a valuable skill.

You learn this with time, but what if you had hi-insight right now?

Wouldn't that be helpful? Yes. That's a hard YES.

Loyalty is one of my core principles and the person I must be loyal to first and foremost is me. That may sound selfish but it is not. Putting myself first in a healthy way so I'm in the best shape possible to reach my goals and care for my family has been a life long learning journey. And yes, I wrote those words and repeat them to myself frequently, like a mantra.

I had a lot of 'unlearning' to do in order to become my true self.

I want to make 8 yr old me proud that I did the work.

80 yr old me is the person I'm heading towards.

So often we worry about what others think. But before everyone else gets to have a say in who and what we are, make sure your voice is the one that's heard.

The information in this book is universal. It is applicable across-the-board. What is common to one is common to all. It leans towards the artist and entrepreneurial spirit, however if you're looking for a way forward, you've found it.

At the end of this book is a section on How It Works and an exercise to get you going. You'll also find a letter from 80 year old me. Flip back and forth as you need, getting the full knowledge of what it is you are now holding in your hand.

Enjoy!

POSTCARDS
FROM MY FUTURE SELF

-1-

Good Morning Sweetheart, 7 is the perfect number and everything is perfectly on track, just as sweetly invigorating as a Bach piece. What is coming is both peaceful, exciting, invigorating and forward growth inducing! There will be stretching, but you will take it in stride. So proud of you girl. So proud. You took courage, you took faith and it is paying off. You've learnt so much along the way. And all that is yours now. No one can take it away. Love from me x

-2-

To Whom It May Concern, The Person Reading this book is an extraordinary talented human being, a multipotentialite! You are gifted with many great talents. Having had a tragically negative and harsh neglectful and humiliating upbringing and early life, you have risen from the ashes, phoenix like. A bright shining golden winged creature, destined for great things. Make no mistake, this bright star is a one off. A Standout. A winner who will win! x

-3-

Dear girl, once again it gives me great joy to write to you and congratulate you on how far you have come. WELL DONE!! Celebrate that. And don't invite your enemies to the party. They will, as they have always done, try to diminish and cloud your results with their bitterness and sickness. You don't owe them or anyone else anything. Stay close to God and walk forward. Well Done.

–4–

Today is a great day to expand. Look how far you've come! What a winner. People are inspired by how you have overcome and continue to grow in new ways. God places His unlimited mind and thoughts in your mind. Your dreams and future are in His Hands. He has never EVER let you down and He won't now. Let go of the outcome. Let go of how you think it's supposed to happen. Let go. Breathe. Expand. Believe. You are all you were made to be and are always moving in ways that lead to good, to love and to abundance and success. Even rest blesses your success. Take it when needed. No guilt. Only progress. Love me.

-5-

Dear girl, it brings me great joy to write you this letter. Let me commend you on your commitment to personal growth and healing. Since your early 20's you have relentlessly pursued this quest. Well done. You are committed to the well being of your family, nurturing and expanding your gifts, being good to those around you and doing things the right way. This kind of honourable action is to be celebrated. Well Done.

-6-

Ok Champion, Listen up! Stay close to your goals. Do not take your eyes off them. Curve balls will come to test you - in fact they are here right now. DO NOT FOLD. Do not bend. There is much at stake.. This is a test. Beware. The flatterer feeds with an empty spoon. Who has your best interests at heart? God. Ultimately. And he trains you in His ways. You are worth more than silver and gold. More than fine jewels. Lift your sights. Lift. Your. Sights.

Now is not the time to quit or take your foot off the gas. I know you are in overwhelm and it feels scary and lonely but this will pass. There will be times of stretching. I believe in you! You will take it in stride. You have overcome SO much! to get to this point. Thing is, it's building up inside you, energy and ideas, and you need to get them out before you explode into pieces. Progress not perfection. A little every day. 80% OK is better than 100% never done.

–8–

Bonjour! I'm writing to wish you a beautiful
day today. A day of miracles and connection,
opportunities and excitement. You have been made
very specifically for such a time as this, with your
gifts and talents. You thought your music days were
over. Not quite. You have been blessed in many
ways and your ability to bless others has just begun.
Andelay!

-9-

Dear One, it's been a while since I've written to you and I know you have my other letters to keep you going. Every word is true. You are unique and your light is changing things around you even now. Even right now. Life is not a straight line. Ride the bumps, the waves. They do not negate the outcomes that await. And await they do. Keep going - sometimes slowly, sometimes quickly. All that is for you has your name on it and it's on it's way to you beautiful one. With love.

-10-

Dearest __(insert your name here)_, It is your future self here. Listen up :- it's coming. Get ready. You have worked very hard on your self and your craft for YEARS. All that is yours has your name on it, and it's on it's way to you. Your enemies are trembling. Sick with their pathological jealousy. They will dig, needle and snipe. Say nothing. Do nothing. They will try to ignore you. Let them. Soar high my darling. Soar high.

-11-

Dear _(insert your name here) _ I am writing to you to encourage you to keep going UNTIL. You are wildly talented and it's just a matter of time until you are recognised in turn. A person would have to be blind, deaf and dumb, or deliberately turning away to not see and acknowledge this FACT. FACT! You have been mightily blessed with creative gifts. You are also a talented writer and speaker and I look forward to that part of your life as it unfolds. xox

-12-

My dearest darling one, I'm so proud of you. Consistently you rise. Consistently you shine. Even your enemies are impressed and have a deep deep respect for you. People are what they are. It's not about you. Move on. Move on towards all that is yours. Let me say, it is moving towards you and quickly. Behold it comes quickly. Be excited. No limits. None. You are magnificent. xox

-13-

My dear girl, finally your enemies and saboteurs
have to face themselves for who and what they
are. As you remove your energy from saving them
and sparing them the emotional results and
consequences of their behaviour and unexamined
lives, they are left with; themselves. Their thoughts
towards you are unfounded and more closely,
projections about them. Leave well enough alone.
You don't owe.

-14-

Hello Dear One, this is your 80 yr old self here, brimming with pride at how far you have come. And look how far you have come! Winner. You arc well on track to fulfil all I wrote about you earlier. Your art is about to take off in ways you never imagined. People are right now gathering towards you behind the scenes to put the wheels on the next phase of your life, your art and your reach and finance. Love from me. Trust.

-15-

Ask : Seek: Knock: ... Do these and you will succeed. Step out. Step out in faith. Boldness has a power all of it's own. I know you feel it mounting. You are a success waiting to happen. It's just a matter of time. Walk straight ahead boldly. Believe. You have asked, now go, seek and knock. The door will be opened. You will find what you are looking for. No doubt. Take courage and go. You can even ask for help to overcome any doubts or unbelief. ASK. Now go!

Take Action. The winds of change and success are on your side.

-16-

Take it easy darling. Go easy. Be kind to you.
Remember - 'I will nurture my artist'. Love yourself
as you would a small child. No good thing ever
emerged from a harsh beating. Life will happen.
God is sovereign. He will do it. Accept it. Allow. Flow.
Do not resist. Surrender. Surrender the outcome.
Do daily, small things and be consistent. Depth is
created little by little, day by day. What you can't see
is more important than what you can see..

You are doing great. Let. It. Be.

-17-

Good morning sweet girl, see I told you things would turn around and they have! Wonderfully. This is your rhythm. Learn it well. You'll understand what to do and what is necessary when your energy takes a turn into dark places. Even there, there is light. You are always moving forward. And you are protected by an unseen detail assigned to you. You are safe xox

-18-

Dearest Darling One, it is your future self here. I have a light in my hand the purpose of which is to guide you to your future. Yes! Your future is bright. Walk towards it as it moves towards you. I know that sometimes you are afraid of how it will all come together. This is normal. Don't think it strange. Keep moving forward. You are more ordered and powerful than you think. Congratulations on doing the very thing you fear. That is the way. Keep going. x

-19-

Dear Girl, you are a beautiful, beautiful woman; both inside and out. You are most singular, outstanding amongst your generation. You have devoted yourself to godliness, raising your family, personal development and healing. AND you have developed and nurtured your gifts and talents to the highest degree. All this you have done with little to no family and adversaries at every turn. Do not, on any front ever sell yourself short. You deserve the best and every success, especially in relationship

-20-

And also! Let me say, that your loyalty, honour and commitment are three of your greatest qualities. Not come about by easily. You were abandoned, but have become committed, you were betrayed but cherish and practise loyalty; You were wrongly shamed and you have alchemized those experiences into honour. These are not small things. You are amazing. Own it. 🩶

-21-

Congratulations! You earned it!! You deserve it!
Claim it baby!! Accept your greatness. You have
worked tirelessly and relentlessly towards this. Don't
you dare dull your shine to keep grizzly, miserly,
stingy, unkind people appeased or happy with the
energy around you. Shine on darling. Ever brighter.
It is your birthright. I can't tell you how proud I am
of you. You do my heart good. Love you longtime. xxx

-22-

You really are something! Sweet girl, take a bow.
Even on slow days you get up and keep going,
waiting, actively patient for either energy or peace
to arrive. And 10 points for being gentle in the
interim. Well done. That's the way - gentle, steady
+ consistent. Work on what you can when you can.
Workouts and accounts are important. Just do
it. Results will follow. As with everything you do.
Results. Will. Follow. xox

-23-

And one more thing:- Your future is bright! Your art is brilliant and people recognise not just the talent and beauty of it but the courage and it gives them hope. Hope that there is courage and beauty and good things in the world. Your art will change peoples lives as much as it's changed yours and you know that's quite a bit. More people love and admire you than you know. But one day you will know.

-24-

Hands off the outcome my love.

TRUST. Your future is as pretty and bright
as this heart 💜

God has shown you time and time again that He is
the master of precision and timing. Keep close by
Him. Your dreams come from God and God has the
power to accomplish them. He is the great Creator.
He did create you and with a purpose in mind that
He is determind to complete and bring to fruition.
Your job is to look good, glow, and walk through that
door. Stay focused, humble & full savage. SMILE!

-25-

Look at you go champion! Day in and day out you put in the work; whether you want to or not. That's what champions are made of and that's what you are. You are an inspiration to many, especially your children. Especially your kids. You have no idea the ripple effect of all that you have done over the last 2 years, what you continue to do and all that you are actuating right now. Well done. Even in the dark of night, keep going. The dawn will break. The tree will fall. Love from me.

-26-

#1 NY Times Best Seller - that's you! #1Amazon Best Seller - That's you!

Viral TED talk. That's you. You are on track. Well done for taking courage. Well done for putting in the work. Well done for commitment + sticking with it, year in and year out. Well done. You have progressively moved forward in spite of your fears and doubts and this is to be applauded. There are 2 angels by your side - One to the left and one to the right. Lean when necessary. Wield that sword.

-27-

You are well on your way to cracking the code. The finance code, the health code and even the reputation code. You are rocketing along towards abundance and success in these areas. Do not doubt it. You have seen for yourself in retrospect, the gold, the light, the vibe shining off you and from within you. Now. Don't take any steps back.That lesson is learnt. Will it be tested? YES!

That's how we know the lesson is over - and on to the next. Your growth rate is exponential.

Well Done. Keep going.

-28-

Alright girl. I get it. It's getting tough. Hang in there.
It's gonna switch, flick, and turn it will.

It will. You have to hang in and keep going. People
are watching. They are waiting to see if, 1.you are for
real. 2. When you might interface with their needs
and 3. Where would be the point where they could
connect. People are not as bold or courageous as you
and are not as courageous as you might think they
are. Give them time. Be patient. Give your self time.
You do need it. ♥ Blessings chase you down.

-29-

Use the dirt! Haters, energy vampires, snarky people, buzz kills, judgmental small minded people, critics its all DIRT! Use it as compost. The mealy mouthed gossips. It's dirt. You are the beautiful pink and yellow flowers that grow from the manure people think they'll ruin you with. You are a beautiful bouquet. All flowers grow from dirt. Use the dirt to grow into the beautiful garden that you are. Don't give up now.

-30-

Good Morning Sweetheart, look how far you have come!! You'll never know all the people you've inspired with your journey so far, but know this; You are on your way to great places, fulfilling dreams, great connections, interesting and valuable friendships and partners. You are valued. You are sort after. People are honoured to be your friend and work with you, to help you along your creative journey. Prepare now: things are about to expand beyond your wildest dreams. You are doing so great!!

-31-

Dear sweet girl, I know. I know. You have so much to offer, so much is admirable - hang in there. Just hang on. Today, rest a little. Do good by you. Let other things fall away. Take 24 hrs off. No thinking hustling, worrying. Hand it over. You'll be on the upswing again soon. All things pass. Your goodness, consistency and talent and hard work, will pay off. Mark my words.

-32-

My dear girl, so much is on it's way to you it's not funny. You have traversed through a tight difficult passage with honour, dignity and credit. You are a credit to yourself, to your family and to God. Well done. As you keep taking right step after right step the power of the future mounts. It's just a matter of time before the bright bright future appears. Before the tree falls. Chop after hit after chop - the tree will fall. Well done.

-33-

Hey There You, you're doing a great job. Just
wanted to say THANKS!

-34-

Can we just stop for a second and acknowledge
what a good parent you are? You continually
put your family 1st, without ignoring your own
needs and progress. This is a tough balance and
you do it well. Never mind x10 that difficulty as
a solo parent. Well done. You are there for them
– physically, emotionally, a listening ear, giving
great encouragement. They know they are greatly
loved. And you mentor them in doing for you. TCB.
Outstanding. Take a bow. xox

-35-

Well well my love, you are learning so much and here's the thing; you do learn and change. So many don't. Give yourself some credit there. Many of the experiences you are now learning from are tests; testing that past lessons or experiences have been alchemized and continue to be. You are seeing people and the world as it is, not as you thought it was, or as you would like it to be. THIS IS HUGE.
WELL DONE xox

-36-

Dear One, today I want you to walk around as if you were me. I want you to pause before you speak. I want you to walk a little slower. That's right. Like that. I want you to accept your greatness. Accept it. This is not about ego or hubris. Quite the opposite. I want you to take up your God given space in the world. This is the very definition of humility.

Be me today, please. xox

-37-

Oh My Dear Sweet Heart, happiness is allowed! In spades. Go for it. You are amazing. You deserve it. You have put in the work. Relentlessly. Now is the time to enjoy. Don't not enjoy it. Embrace it. It is a gift. Not a sin! Your happiness makes others happy. The only people it makes miserable are miserable people. And they will continue to be miserable wether you are happy or not! So you might as well be as happy as you want to be!!!

-38-

Dear one, take the next right step. Give people and
yourself a break. Well done for caring enough to not
let someone stew in a lack of clarity even if it made
you feel vulnerable. Well done. Keep doing that.
And surround yourself with people who reciprocate
clarity. Be me today. Everyday, just a little, be me.
Bullies don't win in the end. They are weak.

-39-

Doing little things daily is how you've made such great progress. Remember that when you get frustrated that big things aren't happening quickly enough. It's the little daily things that add up to the big things eventually. Don't fall off. Don't take your eyes off the prize. The goal is to keep going until and you can only do that, little by little, day by day. Love from me, you are doing GREAT!

-40-

BREATHE. I'm so pleased you check in with me regularly. See how well that works for you? You immediately settle into a stronger, deeper part of your seat. You become unshakeable. This IS who you are. You ARE that person. And the more you check in and practise that, the better you'll become at doing it. It's all gonna work out girl. It's all gonna work out. Mark my words.

-41-

My Dearest Heart, I want YOU TO know that I am so proud of you. You have no idea the energy you are shifting around you for good. People need light and you are a light beam. It gives me great joy to watch you make progress. Know that I am always here. I will never leave you. We will meet at the end of the road. And so until then, take all my words to heart. Read them regularly. Open this book at random pages and take what you need. There's plenty more where this came from. We will never run out of love and abundance. We will never run out of energy and ideas. We will never run out of miracles and connections.

I encourage you to BELIEVE. Daily. Keep doing all that you know to do to stay well: Pray, mediate,write, journal, workout, get sleep, fast weekly and fuel your body with good food. These are the true acts of self love. Surround your self with happy positive people who are like minded and interesting. This alone will keep the darkness at bay. I know you struggle with that at times but your daily affirmations and daily self talk are impactful. They are louder than all other voices if you practise them daily.

So proud of you. So proud.

———

"People like us who believe in physics,
know that the distinction between the
past, the present and the future is only a
stubbornly persistent illusion"

- Albert Einstein

———

Your turn! Here's how to do this.

Writing postcards and letters from your future self, to
you now.

After you've read this book and get a bit of an idea on how it goes,
do the exercise below.

My writing looks and feels like me. Your writing will look and feel
like you.

EXERCISE

One of the best things I ever did was write a letter to my 'now self' from my 'future self', 80 year old me. Every time I do this, it has a profound effect. It sounds hard. It isn't. What will I say? Just get that pen started, the thing will write itself. As you begin to write, a flow arrives that taps into a deep inner wisdom that actually feels as if it's coming from outside yourself and from within, at the same time. I know, it makes no natural, sense. All I know is it works, and that's good enough for me. I know it's connected to my intuition and I know it is fearless and ruthlessly truth telling. No one will ever read it, but you. The good the bad, the difficult and the glory, it will all come out. Intention plays a role. It will reflect the very things going on for you right now, by one step ahead. Be careful not to be you in the present. Allow the inner wisdom that comes from a peaceful place to take over. I wrote a letter from my 80 yr old self to my 50 yr old self and I read it regularly. It puts me on track. It's soothing, humbling and validating. Perhaps it's from the parent I never had. Perhaps its from a wise old loving authentic lady. I can hear and see an older me in her words.

Also, whenever I feel stressed about a situation, anxious in the company of someone, or even at the thought of being in the company of that person; if I'm confused about an issue that doesn't make sense or doesn't add up, or feel that I'm losing it in someway, something has knocked me off balance, unseated me from my centre, I say, (sometimes aloud) " How would future me handle this? How would future me carry herself right now? What would future me think about this situation, this person, this decision, this circumstance"?

And instantly I slow down. Instantly a solid sense of maturity, inner knowing, higher vibration, deep answer, calmness, self realisation and self assuredness both falls on me and wells up from within me. Now I'm a believer, so I think God has something to do with it. I think He is calling me forward towards all I was made to be. That's my true take on all this. You can say, higher power, universe, universal parent, spirit - whoever or whatever you choose to call this power greater than yourself, it is part you and part not you - it is your future you, your inner tutor, connected to the Great Creator Spirit.

So you are going to write a beautiful encouraging, eye opening letter to yourself by hand, from future you. If you're 20 write from 50 year old you. If you're 50 write from 80 year old you. Don't overthink it. You'll find mine at the end of this book. Put it in the snail mail post. What a delight it is when that thing turns up!

Moving on from there, to get a stack going, once a week, write a postcard from future you, to you now. Postcards really work the best. They're punchy, quick and you see the handwriting straight away when it turns up; which again, is a strange delight! And even though you wrote it yourself, once it's in the post, you'll forget what you said. It'll turn up at the perfect time, with just the right piece of love or foresight you need. Right when I need a super piece of encouragement from someone I can fully trust, without reservation, the postcard arrives. It arrives from someone who absolutely has my best interests at heart. No question. If you don't believe in a power outside of yourself or the power of synchronicity, you soon will.

No one, and I mean no one has your back like future you. No spouse, mentor, boss, friend or family member - no one.

Once a week, write yourself a postcard from future you. Just do it. You'll soon have a stack. Each morning in my journaling and meditation time, I pull one out at random, like a lucky dip and read it. Sometimes it's the first thing I read in my morning routine, even before I start journaling because it sets the tone for the day. It works again! And again and again.

HOW IT WORKS

———
❦

80 yr old me looks back on me now.

Me now only has to look to future me by one day, one week or one year to to get a clue and a cue, on how to act, walk, talk and consider herself.

If you consistently hold yourself and command your life, the way future you would, if you consistently do this on a daily basis, the flutter of those little butterfly wings are going to turn into earthquakes felt far across the seas and back again.

The postcards that I write are from 80 year old me, to me now.

She's like a mother, a parent. She speaks to me and considers me the way I speak to my daughter and consider her. I never had such a person and perhaps you never did either. I never had a champion. A person who considered me the ants pants and didn't mind telling me so. Someone who was in no way in competition with me. Someone who doesn't feel the need to one up you or make sure you don't rise too high for their liking.

Everyone needs a person like this to draw the greatness out of them.

Either way, each day at various times, I think to myself, 'how would Future me be doing this right now? how would she carry herself right now'? and I immediately sense the shift of energy around me. Future me, by one day, one week or one year, has a lot to offer, by way of mindset, energy & vibration. Her vibration is slightly higher than mine. She is more calm, less flustered and makes better decisions. She walks a little slower, talks a little less. She doesn't feel the need. She makes decisions based on facts and evidence, not emotions or ego or old programming, which I am apt to do. She is deeply compassionate and understands that in order to give well we must be at our best.

She loves deeply and chooses wisely.

Energy does not lie. If I go too long without considering how future me would carry herself, I begin to feel stagnant or worse, slip backwards into allowing old patterns, mindsets and overwhelming emotions, to steer the ship.

When I think, 'how would future me carry herself right now' - Future me brings me back to base. She is only concerned with me now, me in this very moment. What am I thinking now? What am I feeling now? How is my energy now? She understands that the power of any project or desire or dream or any anything, a relationship, is now. The power and the answer, the ability to shift anything is in the day. It is in the present moment.

When I dream of or worry about tomorrow, she sobers me up to be here now. If I lament the past or go down some, 'wish I did it differently' or, ' why did this happen', rabbit hole she brings me back to the present moment - usually with the gentle words of 'stop fighting yesterday's war, let's get on with today ', and we work on now.

Me now, looks back at me in my 20's and 30's and I see how much time I wasted worrying about things from the past I couldn't change and concerning myself about things in the future I was powerless over.

Postcards From My Future Self

I used up so much energy that could have been way better spent, if I just looked at the day, did the next right thing, and concentrated on what was right in front of me and that which I did have power over - myself: my attitudes, decisions, how I carried myself. Instead I abandoned all that to disassociation in thoughts and feelings, and numbing with over working, over playing, self medicating, ego, fantasy, anything that removed me from the present, the way I was feeling and having to do the actual work, not just the appearance of the work. I did a lot of running around and used up a lot of energy and generated a lot of 'stuff' but I was not present. It was all for some unseen purpose, over there. The disease of over there and someday. I missed my moments. I won't make that mistake again - and I certainly won't make that mistake again with future me guiding and mentoring me on a daily basis.

FINAL THOUGHTS

U nless you are deliberately thinking, 'how does future me hold themselves, how do they walk, how do they talk, how do they think, what do they think, how do they conduct themselves', Unless you are fully awake and aware and cognoscente of these thoughts, you are on auto pilot. You risk slipping back into old versions of yourself, or you are aimlessly moving forward in directions that are not instigated or implemented by you but by others, by circumstances and by your own old programming.

Is that what you want? No. You need to be the boss of you. You need to work on having sovereignty. It is your birthright. Do not be tossed about and triggered by every wind and change, by every relationship or unexpected circumstance and outcome. To become and remain solid in this life is quite the challenge and quite the victory if you are able.

I will end this book, the way it all started for me, with a letter from 80 yr old me.

Thank you for buying and reading this book

I wish you every success in all your endeavours, and who knows maybe our future selves will meet up one day!

LETTER FROM 80 YEAR OLD ME

Dear Deborah

I am you. I am you at 80.

You are now 50

Dear Girl,

You have so much to offer the world. And you are still quite young.

Embrace your beauty, embrace your talent and beautiful spirited heart. Fly High.

The dissenters will disappear into the distant scenery.

At 80 I can see how hard working and talented you are.

You have overcome some terrible circumstances and risen from the rubble.

This frightens people because they don't know what you'll do next, what you'll do with all that power. They are small and visionless.

They don't understand you, or what keeps you going, what powers you.

Pay them no mind. None. Absolutely none.

You will develop a strategy of not thinking about these people.

You will continue to rise regardless.

Keep moving towards your dreams. They will come to pass.

Stay strong in your faith. God is with you Deborah & it is evident.

Even non-believers can see it.

Stay on the path, stay sober, work your recovery.

Don't be afraid, or shy, to say no to people who are not for you.

Get into the habit of only spending your time and effort on that which lights you up.

People will claw at you for time and attention which they interpret as validation.

Don't buy it and don't bite.

Stay aloof from these blood sucking vampires. They bring you no good.

Learn to gravitate to good, true, light, love, warm and genuine support.

Be quick to remove yourself from any toxic situation or person.

Don't worry about the outcome. God will provide.

As you do this consistently, things will get better & better and you'll be dealing with less of these people.

Entertain no nonsense. Don't tell people you are leaving. Just leave.

You owe nobody any explanation whatsoever about anything.

You have earned the right to make choices that 100% bless you, support you and your dreams and goals and one of those goals is to be as far away from these people as possible. They will fade dear girl, they will fade.

Some of them will even become your biggest fans.

Postcards From My Future Self

Know this : you are on the right path.

God has wonderful surprises, outcomes & opportunities up ahead for you that you haven't even thought of. Stay humble; it is attractive and magnetic.

Don't boast. Let others do that for you.

Don't take ill will to heart. It's not about you.

They will blow off like mist. Today you, tomorrow someone else.

You have raised your children well & they will give you years of joy, love, blessing and support. They are proud of you and love you very much.

You are admired by people you don't know, don't yet know, and who don't show it.

Don't focus on that, just keep being you.

Don't chase glory, accolades and praise. Just keep being you.

It will all work out for good in the end.

You are now 80 & deeply satisfied with your life, how you turned things around, and where you're at now and this is great reward; a great life outcome and satisfaction that few get to experience. You gave everything your best shot and you have no regrets about doing that. You made courageous choices and they paid off.

Your loving faith filled godly life, has been the making of you.

You are deeply loved and blessed

Love Deborah @ 80.

ABOUT THE AUTHOR

Deborah Dicembre is an award winning musician. Her extensive body of work can be found on debdicembremusic.com and purchased on iTunes. She is a speaker and writer, working with high school girls at risk and women at wellness seminars and in relationship recovery. Deborah recently began debdicembrebooks.com to collate her articles in one place. Dicembre is an accomplished abstract artist having had her first solo show in August 2022 at Fern Street Gallery, Gerringong NSW Australia. She has also designed a collection of abstract wall art. Her art can be found on deborahdicembre.com.

Deborah's next body of work 'Master Peace_alchemy', will be shown in November 2023

Deborah is a mother of two teenagers and lives on the south east coast of Australia

Made in the USA
Coppell, TX
27 February 2023

13496593R00036